FaithWords
Hachette Book Group
237 Park Avenue
New York, NY 10169

Visit our Web site at www.faithwords.com.

Printed in the United States of America

First Warner Faith Edition: October 2002
10 9 8 7 6 5

The FaithWords name and logo are trademarks of Hachette Book Group.

ISBN 978-0-446-53208-2
LCCN: 2002110838

NEVER LOSE HEART

Encouragement for the Journey

JOYCE MEYER

FaithWords

NEW YORK BOSTON NASHVILLE

CONTENTS

WHEN
YOU FEEL
STRESSED

*Peace comes to every situation
when we choose to listen to and obey
the Lord. We must follow Wisdom
to enjoy blessed lives.*

GOD'S WORD FOR YOU

Be anxious for nothing, but in everything by prayer and supplication with thanksgiving let your requests be made known to God.

And the peace of God, which surpasses all comprehension, will guard your hearts and your minds in Christ Jesus.

PHILIPPIANS 4:6-7 NASB

one

WHEN YOU
FEEL STRESSED

few years ago, I went to a doctor because I was constantly sick. He told me the symptoms were the result of being under stress. I was sleeping wrong, eating improperly, and pushing myself harder and harder—all in the name of working for the Lord.

The word *stress* was originally an engineering term used to refer to the amount of force that a beam or other physical support could bear without collapsing under the strain. In our time, stress has been expanded to include mental and emotional tension.

Stress is a normal part of everyone's life. God has created us to withstand a certain amount of pressure and tension. The problem comes when we push beyond our limitations and head toward doing permanent damage to ourselves.

Peace is meant to be the normal condition for every believer in Jesus Christ. He is the Prince of Peace, and in Jesus we find our own inheritance of peace. It is a gift from the Holy Spirit, which He gives as we live in obedience to His Word.

The peace Jesus gives operates in good times or bad,
when you are abounding or being abased.
His peace operates in the middle of a storm.

GOD'S WORD FOR YOU

Do you not know that your body is the temple (the very sanctuary) of the Holy Spirit Who lives within you, Whom you have received [as a Gift] from God? You are not your own,

You were bought with a price [purchased with a preciousness and paid for, made His own]. So then, honor God and bring glory to Him in your body.

1 CORINTHIANS 6:19-20

❧

Have you not known? Have you not heard? The everlasting God, the Lord, the Creator of the ends of the earth, does not faint or grow weary; there is no searching of His understanding.

He gives power to the faint and weary, and to him who has no might He increases strength [causing it to multiply and making it to abound].

ISAIAH 40:28-29

REFRESH THE WEARY

The first key to handling or overcoming stress is to recognize or admit we are under it. Though I was constantly having headaches, backaches, stomachaches, neck aches, and all the other symptoms of stress, I found it very difficult to admit that I was pushing too hard physically, mentally, emotionally, and spiritually. I was doing the work I felt God wanted me to do without actually seeking Him to find out which work He wanted me to do, when He wanted me to do it, and how much of it. If we abuse ourselves, we will suffer the consequences.

Although the Lord gives power to the faint and weary, if you are worn out from continually exceeding your physical limitations, you need physical rest. The Lord may mercifully give you supernatural energy in particular instances, but you are in disobedience when you abuse your body, the temple of the Holy Spirit.

If you want God to flow and work through you, you need to take care of your body so God can use you. If you wear out your body, you don't have a spare in the drawer somewhere to pull out!

The anointing of God lifts when you operate outside of His promptings.

GOD'S WORD FOR YOU

I, Wisdom [from God], make prudence my dwelling, and I find out knowledge and discretion.

PROVERBS 8:12

❧

The Wisdom (godly Wisdom, which is comprehensive insight into the ways and purposes of God] of the prudent is to understand his way. . . .

PROVERBS 14:8

❧

RUDENCE

A word you don't hear very much teaching about is "prudence." In the Scriptures "prudence" or "prudent" means being good stewards of the gifts God has given us to use. Those gifts include time, energy, strength, and health as well as material possessions. They include our bodies as well as our minds and spirits.

Just as each one of us has been given a different set of gifts, each of us has been given a different ability to manage those gifts. Some of us are better able to manage ourselves than are others.

Each of us needs to know how much we are able to handle. We need to be able to recognize when we are reaching "full capacity" or "overload." Instead of pushing ourselves into overload to please others, satisfy our own desires, or reach our personal goals, we need to listen to the Lord and obey Him. We must follow Wisdom to enjoy blessed lives.

Nobody can remove all the stressors, the things causing or increasing stress, in our lives. For that reason, each of us must be *prudent* to identify and recognize the stressors that affect us most and learn how to respond to them with the right action.

God is good, and He wants you to believe that He has a good plan for your life, and that He is working in your situation.

GOD'S WORD FOR YOU

If you will listen diligently to the voice of the Lord your God, being watchful to do all His commandments which I command you this day, the Lord your God will set you high above all the nations of the earth.

And the Lord shall make you the head, and not the tail; and you shall be above only, and you shall not be beneath. . . .

DEUTERONOMY 28:1, 13

. . . now we serve not under [obedience to] the old code of written regulations, but [under obedience to the promptings] of the Spirit in newness [of life].

ROMANS 7:6

RELIEVING STRESS

When I began to prepare this message on stress, I asked the Lord to show me how He wanted me to present the material. The answer He gave me is a message, a word, from the heart of the Father for the Body of Christ for this hour, this season.

Another important key to relieving stress is *obedience*.

We may have stress, but we will be on *top* of it, not *under* it. There is a big difference between being *under* stress and being on *top* of a situation!

All of us have situations that come our way we don't like. But, with the power of God, we can go through those circumstances stress free.

Even though, like the people in the world, we will sometimes experience stressful times, if we are obedient to God's Word and to His promptings, we can be on top of stress and not under it.

Do you believe that God is leading you into a place of victory and triumph, not into a place of defeat? Your answer as a child of God and believer in Jesus Christ would be yes! If we believers would listen to everything the Lord tells us and obey Him, we would not get into that state of defeat so often.

Simply obeying the promptings of the Holy Spirit will often relieve stress quickly.

GOD'S WORD FOR YOU

Do you not know that if you continually surrender yourselves to anyone to do his will, you are the slaves of him whom you obey, whether that be to sin, which leads to death, or to obedience which leads to righteousness (right doing and right standing with God)?

ROMANS 6:16

Now therefore, if you will obey My voice in truth and keep My covenant, then you shall be My own peculiar possession and treasure from among and above all peoples; for all the earth is Mine.

EXODUS 19:5

God's Anointing Is on Obedience

God's grace and power are available for us to use. God enables us or gives us an anointing of the Holy Spirit to do what *He* tells us to do. Sometimes after He has prompted us to go another direction, we still keep pressing on with our original plan. If we are doing something He has not approved, He is under no obligation to give us the energy to do it. We are functioning in our own strength rather than under the control of the Holy Spirit. Then we get so frustrated, stressed, or burned out, we lose our self-control, simply by ignoring the promptings of the Spirit.

Many people are stressed and burned out from going their own way instead of God's way. They end up in stressful situations when they go a different direction from the one God prompted. Then they burn out in the midst of the disobedience and, struggling to finish what they started outside of God's direction, beg God to anoint them.

God is merciful, and He helps us in the midst of our mistakes. But He is not going to give us strength and energy to disobey Him continually. We can avoid many stressful situations and living "tied up in knots" simply by obeying the Holy Spirit's promptings moment by moment.

Obeying Him in the little things makes a major difference in keeping stress out of our life.

GOD'S WORD FOR YOU

Let be and be still, and know (recognize and understand) that I am God. I will be exalted among the nations! I will be exalted in the earth!

PSALM 46:10

❧

Lean on, trust in, and be confident in the Lord with all your heart and mind and do not rely on your own insight or understanding.

In all your ways know, recognize, and acknowledge Him, and He will direct and make straight and plain your paths.

PROVERBS 3:5-6

BE STILL AND KNOW GOD

One of the main reasons so many of us are burned out and stressed out is that we don't know how to be still, to "know" God and "acknowledge" Him. When we spend time with Him, we learn to hear His voice. When we acknowledge Him, He directs our paths. We need to learn to be quiet inside and stay in that peaceful state so that we are always ready to hear the Lord's voice.

Many people today run from one thing to the next. Because their minds don't know how to be still, they don't know how to be still.

For a long time I felt I had to find something to do every evening. I had to be involved and a part of whatever was going on. I thought I couldn't afford to miss anything because I didn't want anything to go on that I didn't know about. I couldn't just sit and be still. I had to be up doing something. I was not a human being—I was a human doing.

We need to be careful to submit our ideas and plans to God, then slow down and wait. Make sure there is a sense of peace to go along with the plans and ideas. Ask the Lord for His will in your life, then be still and know that He is God.

God gives His highest and best to those whose trust is in Him. Be still and let Him show Himself strong in your life.

GOD'S WORD FOR YOU

Peace I leave with you; My [own] peace I now give and bequeath to you. Not as the world gives do I give to you. Do not let your hearts be troubled, neither let them be afraid. [Stop allowing yourselves to be agitated and disturbed; and do not permit yourselves to be fearful and intimidated and cowardly and unsettled.]

JOHN 14:27

And let the peace (soul harmony which comes) from Christ rule (act as umpire continually) in your hearts [deciding and settling with finality all questions that arise in your minds, in that peaceful state].

COLOSSIANS 3:15

Jesus, Our Prince of Peace

When we are all stressed out, we would like to eliminate the causes of the problems, but the source of stress is not really difficulties, circumstances, and situations. Stress comes from approaching problems with the world's perspective rather than faith in Jesus Christ, the Prince of Peace.

It was Jesus' blood that bought our peace, but the price we must pay for peace is a willingness to change our approach to life. We will never enjoy peace without a willingness to adjust and adapt ourselves. We must be willing to sacrifice worry and reasoning if we are to know peace. We cannot have anxiety, frustration, or rigid, legalistic attitudes and enjoy the peace of God.

Even though we will have disturbing issues to deal with, we can have Jesus' peace because He has "overcome the world" and "deprived" the world of its "power to harm" us. He left us with the power to "stop allowing" ourselves "to be agitated and disturbed"! Peace is available, but we must choose it!

The Prince of Peace, Jesus, Who lives inside those of us who have received Him, knows and will reveal to us the specific actions we need to take in every situation to lead us into peace.

It is absolutely amazing what we can accomplish in Christ if we live one day at a time in His peace.

GOD'S WORD FOR YOU

*Even when we were dead (slain) by [our own]
shortcomings and trespasses, He made us alive together in
fellowship and in union with Christ; [He gave us the very
life of Christ Himself, the same new life with which He
quickened Him, for] it is by grace (His favor and mercy
which you did not deserve) that you are saved (delivered
from judgment and made partakers of Christ's salvation).*

EPHESIANS 2:5

❧

*But He gives us more and more grace (power of the
Holy Spirit, to meet this evil tendency and all others fully).
. . . God sets Himself against the proud . . . but gives
grace [continually] to the lowly (those who are humble
enough to receive it).*

JAMES 4:6

22

WORKS VERSUS GRACE

We get so frustrated because we are trying to live by *works* a life that was brought into being and designed by God to be lived by *grace*. The more we try to figure out what to do to solve our dilemma, the more confused, upset, and frustrated we become.

When you get into a frustrating situation, just stop and say, "O Lord, give me grace." Then believe that God has heard your prayer and is answering that prayer and working out that situation.

Faith is the channel through which you and I receive the grace of God. If we try to do things on our own without being open to receive the grace of God, then no matter how much faith we may have, we will still not receive what we are asking of God.

A long time ago I wrote up this statement and stuck it on my refrigerator:

Works of the flesh = Frustration.

If you can learn this principle, you will soon overcome the evil tendency to become frustrated.

We need to trust in and rely on the grace of God. He knows what we are facing in every situation of life, and He will work out things for the best if we will trust Him enough to allow Him to do so.

❧

Remember, it is not by power or by might, but by the Spirit that we win the victory over our enemy.

GOD'S WORD FOR YOU

Now unto him that is able to do exceeding abundantly above all that we ask or think, according to the power that worketh in us.

EPHESIANS 3:20 KJV

 God Is Able

This is a powerful Scripture that tells us that our God is able—able to do far above and beyond anything that you and I can ever dare to hope, ask, or even think. We need to pray, to do the asking in faith and in trust. But it is God Who does the work, not us. How does He do it? *According to* [or by] *the power* [or grace of God] *that worketh in us.* Whatever you and I receive from the Lord is directly related to the amount of grace we learn to receive.

I was putting unbelievable stress on myself trying to change. I was under tremendous condemnation because every message I heard seemed to be telling me to change, yet I couldn't change no matter how hard I tried, believed, or confessed. I was in a terrible mess because I saw all the things about me that needed to be changed, but I was powerless to bring about those changes.

The Lord has to be our Source and our Supply. He is the only One who can bring about changes in our lives. I had to learn to say, "Father, although I am not worthy of Your help, I know that the changes You want in my life are not going to work unless You add the power."

God promises to strengthen us in our weaknesses if we trust Him and turn to Him. God's grace will be sufficient in our need.

WHEN
YOU FEEL
DISCOURAGED

*Happiness and joy do not come
from the outside. They come
from within. They are a conscious
decision, a deliberate choice, one that
we make ourselves each day we live.*

GOD'S WORD FOR YOU

[What, what would have become of me] had I not believed that I would see the Lord's goodness in the land of the living!

Wait and hope for and expect the Lord; be brave and of good courage and let your heart be stout and enduring. Yes, wait for and hope for and expect the Lord.

PSALM 27:13-14

❧

For I know the thoughts and plans that I have for you, says the Lord, thoughts and plans for welfare and peace and not for evil, to give you hope in your final outcome.

JEREMIAH 29:11

t w o

WHEN YOU FEEL DISCOURAGED

e have all been disappointed at some time. It would be surprising if we went through the week without encountering some kind of disappointment. We are "appointed" (set in a certain direction) for something to happen a certain way, and when it doesn't happen that way, we become "dis-appointed."

Disappointment not dealt with turns into discouragement. If we stay discouraged very long, we are liable to become devastated, and devastation leaves us unable to handle anything.

Many devastated Christians are lying along the roadside of life because they have not learned how to handle disappointment. The devastation they are experiencing now most likely began with a minor disappointment that was not dealt with properly.

It is not God's will for us to live disappointed, devastated, or oppressed! When we become "disappointed," we must learn to become "re-appointed" to keep from becoming discouraged, then devastated.

When we learn to place our hope and confidence in Jesus the Rock (1 Corinthians 10:4) and resist the devil at the onset, we can live in the joy and peace of the Lord, free from discouragement.

Choose to aggressively withstand the devil so you can live in the fullness of life God has provided for you through His Son Jesus Christ.

GOD'S WORD FOR YOU

. . . for God selected (deliberately chose) what in
the world is foolish to put the wise to shame, and what
the world calls weak to put the strong to shame.

And God also selected (deliberately chose) what in
the world is lowborn and insignificant and branded and
treated with contempt, even the things that are nothing,
that He might depose and bring to nothing the things
that are,

So that no mortal man should [have pretense for
glorying and] boast in the presence of God.

1 CORINTHIANS 1:27-29

$\mathcal{G}$OD CHOOSES THE UNLIKELY

When you feel discouraged, remember that God chose you for His very own purpose, however unlikely a candidate you feel. By doing so, He has placed before you a wide open door to show you His boundless grace, mercy, and power to change your life.

When God uses any one of us, though we may all feel inadequate and unworthy, we realize that our source is not in ourselves but in Him alone: "[This is] because the foolish thing [that has its source in] God is wiser than men, and the weak thing [that springs] from God is stronger than men" (1 Corinthians 1:25).

Each of us has a destiny, and there is absolutely no excuse not to fulfill it. We cannot use our weakness as an excuse because God says that His strength is made perfect in weakness (2 Corinthians 12:9). We cannot use the past as an excuse because God tells us through the apostle Paul that if any person is in Christ, he is a new creature; old things have passed away, and all things have become new (2 Corinthians 5:17).

Spend some time with yourself and take an inventory of how you feel about yourself. What is your image of yourself? Do you see yourself re-created in God's image, resurrected to a brand-new life that is just waiting for you to claim it?

Each of us can succeed at being everything God intends us to be.

GOD'S WORD FOR YOU

. . . the Word of God . . . is effectually at work in you who believe [exercising its superhuman power in those who adhere to and trust in and rely on it].

1 THESSALONIANS 2:13

We Are a "Work in Progress"

I encourage you to say every day, *"God is working in me right now—He is changing me!"* Speak out of your mouth what the Word says, not what you feel. When we incessantly talk about how we feel, it is difficult for the Word of God to work in us effectively.

As we step out to be all we can be in Christ, we will make some mistakes—everyone does. But it takes the pressure off of us when we realize that God is expecting us to do the best we can. He is not expecting us to be perfect (totally without flaw). If we were as perfect as we try to be, we would not need a Savior. I believe God will always leave a certain number of defects in us, just so we will know how much we need Jesus every single day.

I am not a perfect preacher. There are times when I say things wrong, times when I believe I have heard from God and find out I was hearing from myself. There are many times when I fall short of perfection. I don't have perfect faith, a perfect attitude, perfect thoughts, and perfect ways.

Jesus knew that would happen to all of us. That is why He stands in the gap between God's perfection and our imperfection. He *continually* intercedes for us because we *continually* need it (Hebrews 7:25).

We do not have to believe that God accepts us only if we perform perfectly. We can believe the truth that He accepts us "in the Beloved."

GOD'S WORD FOR YOU

Fight the good fight of the faith; lay hold of the eternal life to which you were summoned and [for which] you confessed the good confession [of faith] before many witnesses.

1 TIMOTHY 6:12

 Be a Fighter

To be aggressive is to be a fighter. Just as the apostle Paul said that he had fought the good fight of faith (2 Timothy 4:7), so he instructed his young disciple Timothy to fight the good fight of faith. In the same way, we are to fight the good fight of faith in our daily lives as we struggle against spiritual enemies in high places and in our own mind and heart.

One part of fighting the good fight of faith is being able to recognize the enemy. As long as we are passive, Satan will torment us. Nothing is going to change about our situation if all we do is just sit and wish things were different. We have to take action. Too often we don't move against the enemy when he comes against us with discouragement or fear or doubt or guilt. We just draw back into a corner somewhere and let him beat us up.

You and I are not supposed to be punching bags for the devil; instead, we are supposed to be fighters.

Now the devil wants us to fight in the natural with everybody around us. But God wants us to forget all the junk that Satan stirs up within us to get us riled up against other people. Instead, He wants us to fight against the spiritual enemies who try to war over our lives and steal our peace and joy.

Come against Satan when he is trying to get a foothold, and he will never get a stronghold.

GOD'S WORD FOR YOU

For as many as are the promises of God, they all find their Yes [answer] in Him [Christ]. For this reason we also utter the Amen (so be it) to God through Him [in His Person and by His agency] to the glory of God.

2 CORINTHIANS 1:20

CONFIDENCE IN JESUS

In several places in the Bible, for example in
1 Corinthians 10:4, Jesus is referred to as the Rock.
The apostle Paul goes on to tell us in Colossians 2:7
that we are to be rooted and grounded in Him.

If we get our roots wrapped around Jesus Christ, we
are in good shape. But if we get them wrapped around
anything or anyone else, we are in trouble.

Nothing nor no one is going to be as solid and
dependable and immovable as Jesus. That's why I don't
want people to get rooted and grounded in me or my
ministry. I want to point people to Jesus. I know that
ultimately I will fail them in some way, just as I know
they will ultimately fail me.

That's the problem with us humans; we are always
liable to failure. But Jesus Christ isn't. Put your hope
wholly and unchangeably in Him. Not in man, not in
circumstances, not in anything or anyone else.

If you don't put your hope and faith in the Rock of
your salvation, you are headed for disappointment,
which leads to discouragement and devastation. We
should have so much confidence in God's love for us
that no matter what comes against us, we know deep
inside that we are more than conquerors.

❧

*We need to come to a state of utter bankruptcy in our
own ability apart from Christ. Without God, we are
helpless; with Him nothing is impossible to us.*

GOD'S WORD FOR YOU

. . . let us run with patient endurance and steady and active persistence the appointed course of the race that is set before us.

Looking away [from all that will distract] to Jesus, Who is the Leader and the Source of our faith [giving the first incentive for our belief] and is also its Finisher [bringing it to maturity and perfection]. He, for the joy [of obtaining the prize] that was set before Him, endured the cross, despising and ignoring the shame, and is now seated at the right hand of the throne of God.

Just think of Him Who endured from sinners such grievous opposition and bitter hostility against Himself [reckon up and consider it all in comparison with your trials], so that you may not grow weary or exhausted, losing heart and relaxing and fainting in your minds.

HEBREWS 12:1-3

KEEP ON LOOKING TO JESUS

It does not take any special talent to give up and lie down on the side of the road of life and say, "I quit." Any unbeliever can do that.

You don't have to be a Christian to be a quitter. But once you get hold of Jesus, or better yet when He gets hold of you, He begins to pump strength and energy and courage into you, and something strange and wonderful begins to happen. He won't let you quit!

I used to want to give up and quit. But now I get out of bed and start each day afresh and anew. I begin my day by praying and reading the Bible and speaking the Word, seeking after God.

The devil may be screaming in my ear, "That's not doing you one bit of good. You've been doing that for years and look what it's got you—you still have trouble."

That's when I say, "Shut up, devil! The Bible says that I am to look to Jesus and follow His example. He is my Leader, the Source and Finisher of my faith.

You and I need to make a decision today that, come what may, we are going to keep pressing on, looking to Jesus, no matter what.

GOD'S WORD FOR YOU

Do not fret or have any anxiety about anything, but in every circumstance and in everything, by prayer and petition (definite requests), with thanksgiving, continue to make your wants known to God.

And God's peace [shall be yours, that tranquil state of a soul assured of its salvation through Christ, and so fearing nothing from God and being content with its earthly lot of whatever sort that is, that peace] which transcends all understanding shall garrison and mount guard over your hearts and minds in Christ Jesus.

PHILIPPIANS 4:6-7

EDITATE ON THE THINGS OF GOD

If you don't want to be devastated by discouragement, then don't meditate on your disappointments.

Did you know that your feelings are hooked up to your thinking? If you don't think that is true, just take about twenty minutes or so and think about nothing but your problems. I can assure you that by the end of that time your feelings and maybe even your countenance will have changed.

I got up one day thinking about a problem I had. Suddenly the Spirit of the Lord spoke to me. He said to me, "Joyce, are you going to fellowship with your problem or with Me?"

When you get disappointed, don't sit around and feel sorry for yourself. As bad as things may seem, we still have a choice. We can choose to fellowship with our problems or fellowship with God.

We can allow our thoughts to dwell on the bad things until we become totally discouraged and devastated, or we can focus our attention on all the good things that have happened to us in our life—and on all the blessings that God still has in store for us in the days ahead.

Our thoughts are silent words that only we and the Lord hear, but those words affect our inner man, our health, our joy, and our attitude.

GOD'S WORD FOR YOU

Catch the foxes for us, the little foxes that are ruining the vineyards. . . .

SONG OF SOLOMON 2:15 NASB

CATCH THE FOXES

Little disappointments can create frustration, which in turn may lead to bigger problems that can produce a great deal of damage.

Besides the huge disappointments that occur when we fail to get the job promotion or house we wanted, we can become just as upset by minor annoyances. For example, suppose someone is supposed to meet you for lunch and fails to show up. Or suppose you make a special trip to the mall to buy something at a discount, but it's all sold out.

All these kinds of frustrations are actually minor, but they can add up to cause a lot of grief. That's why we have to know how to handle them and keep them in perspective. Otherwise, they can get out of hand and be blown up all out of proportion.

We have to be on our guard against the little foxes that destroy the vineyards, because all together they can do just as much damage as the serious disappointments that often accompany them.

We must learn to do as Paul did in the book of Acts when the serpent attached itself to his hand—he simply shook it off (Acts 28:1-5)! If we practice dealing quickly with disappointments as they come, they will not pile up into a mountain of devastation.

Victory is not the absence of problems;
it is the presence of God's power.

GOD'S WORD FOR YOU

The mystery of which was hidden for ages and generations [from angels and men], but is now revealed to His holy people (the saints),

To whom God was pleased to make known how great for the Gentiles are the riches of the glory of this mystery, which is Christ within and among you, the Hope of [realizing the] glory.

COLOSSIANS 1:26-27

CHRIST IN YOU, THE HOPE OF GLORY

You and I can only realize and experience the glory of God on our lives because of Christ in us. He is our hope of seeing better things.

The glory of God is His manifested excellence. As the children of God, we have a blood-bought right to experience the best God has planned for us. Satan furiously fights the plan of God in each of our lives, and his primary weapon is deception. When we are deceived, we believe something that is not true.

When we look at ourselves and our own ability, we feel defeated, but remembering that Christ lives in us is our hope of realizing the glory. It keeps us encouraged enough to press on toward better things. We limit ourselves when we look to ourselves alone and fail to see Jesus.

The Lord has destined His Church for glory. He is coming back for a glorious Church (Ephesians 5:27). God's glory can be manifested in us and on us, but only as we believe it is possible.

*God is looking for someone who will believe
and receive. He is waiting to manifest His glory
—to you and through you!*

WHEN
YOU FEEL
WORRIED

God has a secret place
of abiding where worry
vanishes and peace reigns.

GOD'S WORD FOR YOU

Humble yourselves therefore under the mighty hand of God, that he may exalt you in due time:

Casting all your care upon him; for he careth for you.

1 PETER 5:6-7 KJV

❧

The Spirit of the Lord God is upon me, because the Lord has anointed and qualified me. . . . To grant [consolation and joy] to those who mourn in Zion—to give them an ornament (a garland or diadem) of beauty instead of ashes ["beauty for ashes" KJV].

ISAIAH 61:1, 3

three

WHEN YOU FEEL WORRIED

od wants to take care of us, but in order to let Him, *we* must stop taking the care. Many people want God to take care of them while they are worrying or trying to figure out an answer instead of waiting for God's direction. They are actually wallowing around in their "ashes," but they still want God to give them beauty. In order for God to give us the beauty, we must give Him the "ashes."

We give Him our cares by trusting that He can and will take care of us. Hebrews 4:3 says: "For we who have believed (adhered to and trusted in and relied on God) do enter that rest. . . ."

We enter into the Lord's rest through believing. Worry is the opposite of faith. Worry steals our peace, physically wears us out, and can even make us sick. If we are worrying, we are not trusting God, and we are not entering God's rest.

What a great trade! You give God ashes, and He gives you beauty. You give Him all your worries and concerns, and He gives you protection, stability, a place of refuge and fullness of joy—the privilege of being cared for by Him.

Jesus did not worry,
and we do not have to worry either.

GOD'S WORD FOR YOU

He who dwells in the secret place of the Most High
shall remain stable and fixed under the shadow of the
Almighty [Whose power no foe can withstand].

PSALM 91:1

ABIDING IN PROTECTION

God has a secret place where we can dwell in peace and safety.

The secret place is the place of rest in God, a place of peace and comfort in Him. This secret place is a "spiritual place" where worry vanishes and peace reigns. It is the place of God's presence. When we spend time praying and seeking God and dwelling in His presence, we are in the secret place.

When you and I *dwell in Christ* or *dwell in the secret place*, we do not just visit there occasionally, we take up permanent residence there.

The secret place is a hiding place, a private place, or a place of refuge. It is the place we run to when we are hurting, overwhelmed, or feeling faint. It is the place we run to when we are being mistreated or persecuted, when we are in great need, or when we feel we just cannot take it anymore.

We need to be firmly planted in God. We need to know the Source of our help in every situation and in every circumstance. We need to have our own secret place of peace and security. We need to rely on God and trust Him completely.

God wants us to take refuge under the protective shadow of His wings. He wants us to run to Him!

GOD'S WORD FOR YOU

Therefore do not worry and be anxious, saying, What are we going to have to eat? or, What are we going to have to drink? or, What are we going to have to wear?

For the Gentiles (heathen) wish for and crave and diligently seek all these things, and your heavenly Father knows well that you need them all.

MATTHEW 6:31-32

Don't Be Anxious

The problem with worry is that it causes us to start saying: "What are we going to have to eat? What are we going to have to drink? What are we going to have to wear?" In other words, "What are we going to do if God doesn't come through for us?"

Instead of calming our fears and removing our worries, we begin to fret and fuss with the words of our mouth, which only makes them even more deeply ingrained.

The problem with this way of doing things is that it is the way people act who don't know they have a heavenly Father. But you and I do know we have a heavenly Father, so we need to act like it.

Jesus assures us that our heavenly Father knows all our needs before we ask Him. So why should we worry about them? Instead, we need to focus our attention on the things that are much more important—the things of God.

Seek first the Kingdom of God
and His righteousness; then all these
other things we need will be added to us.

GOD'S WORD FOR YOU

Only it must be in faith that he asks with no wavering (no hesitating, no doubting). For the one who wavers (hesitates, doubts) is like the billowing surge out at sea that is blown hither and thither and tossed by the wind.

For truly, let not such a person imagine that he will receive anything [he asks for] from the Lord.

JAMES 1:6-7

STAY IN THE POSITIVE

If we take our concerns to the Lord in prayer and then continue to worry about them, we are mixing a positive and a negative force. Prayer is a positive force, and worry is a negative force. If we add them together, we come up with zero. I don't know about you, but I don't want to have zero power, so I try not to mix prayer and worry.

God spoke to me one time and said, "Many people operate with zero power because they are always mixing the positives and the negatives. They have a positive confession for a little while, then a negative confession for a little while. They pray for a little while, then they worry for a little while. They trust for a little while, then they worry for a little while. As a result, they just go back and forth, never really making any progress."

Let's not magnify the bad—let's magnify the good! Let's make it larger by talking about it, by being positive in our thoughts, in our attitudes, in our outlook, in our words, and in our actions.

Why not make a decision to stay in the positive by trusting God and refusing to worry?

Practice being positive in each situation that arises. Even if whatever is taking place at the moment is not so good, expect God to bring good out of it.

GOD'S WORD FOR YOU

Let the redeemed of the Lord say so, whom He has delivered from the hand of the adversary.

PSALM 107:2

❧

For [then] He will deliver you from the snare of the fowler and from the deadly pestilence.

[Then] He will cover you with His pinions, and under His wings shall you trust and find refuge; His truth and His faithfulness are a shield and a buckler.

PSALM 91:3-4

If You're Redeemed, Say So!

When you realize that the devil is trying to distract you, don't just sit around and let him beat you up with worry and negative thoughts. Open your mouth and begin to confess your authority in Christ.

Sometimes while I am preparing to speak at a church or seminar, negative thoughts will begin to bombard me. At those times I encourage myself with my own mouth and say out loud, "Everything is going to be all right."

Satan places anxious and worried thoughts in our minds, sometimes actually "bombarding" our minds with them. He hopes we will receive them and begin "saying" them out of our mouths. If we do, he then has material to actually create the circumstances in our lives he has been giving us anxious thoughts about.

Once I recognized those anxious thoughts and evil forebodings and took authority over them, God began to bring some deliverance to my life so I could start to enjoy it.

Don't be the devil's mouthpiece.

Find out what God's Word promises you and begin to declare His two-edged sword (Hebrews 4:12).

❧

*As we speak the Word out of our mouths
in faith, we wield a mighty two-edged sword
that destroys the enemy.*

GOD'S WORD FOR YOU

Beloved, we are [even here and] now God's children;
it is not yet disclosed (made clear) what we shall be
[hereafter], but we know that when He comes and is
manifested, we shall [as God's children] resemble and be
like Him, for we shall see Him just as He [really] is.

1 JOHN 3:2

Live in the Now

In reality, the choices we make today will determine whether we will enjoy the moment or waste it by worrying. Sometimes we end up missing the moment of today because we are too concerned about tomorrow. We need to keep our mind focused on what God wants us to be doing now.

God gave me a definition of anxiety: "Anxiety is caused by trying to mentally or emotionally get into things that are not here yet (the future) or things that have already been (the past)."

One of the things that we need to understand is that God wants us to learn how to be *now* people. For example, 2 Corinthians 6:2 KJV says, "Behold, now is the day of salvation," and Hebrews 4:7 says, "Today, if you would hear His voice and when you hear it, do not harden your hearts."

We need to learn to live now. Often we spend our mental time in the past or the future. When we don't really give ourselves to what we are doing at the moment, we become prone to anxiety. If we will live in the now, we will find the Lord there with us. Regardless of what situations life brings our way, He has promised never to leave us or forsake us but to always be with us and help us (Hebrews 13:5; Matthew 28:20).

Don't waste your precious "now" worrying about yesterday or tomorrow.

GOD'S WORD FOR YOU

But be doers of the Word [obey the message], and not merely listeners to it, betraying yourselves [into deception by reasoning contrary to the Truth].

JAMES 1:22

GIVE UP EXCESSIVE REASONING

Are you always trying to figure everything out? Many of us have fallen into that ditch. Instead of casting our care upon the Lord, we go through life carrying every bit of it.

When we try to figure everything out, we are exalting our reasoning above God's thoughts. We are placing our ways higher than His ways. When God revealed to me that I had to give up excessive reasoning that was contrary to the truth, it was a real challenge. I couldn't stand it if I did not have everything figured out.

For example, God told us to do some things in our ministry several years ago that I didn't have the slightest idea how to go about doing. But God never called me to figure out exactly how to accomplish everything He asked me to do. He called me to seek *Him* rather than the answer to my problems, then obey what He told me to do.

When we worry, we lose our peace, and when we try to figure everything out, we fall into confusion. Confusion is the result of reasoning with our own understanding when we should be trusting in the Lord with all our heart to make the way for us according to His plan. When we trust that His thoughts are higher than our thoughts, we stop confusion before it starts.

*God's peace is always available,
but we must choose it.*

GOD'S WORD FOR YOU

So trust in the Lord (commit yourself to Him, lean on Him, hope confidently in Him) forever; for the Lord God is an everlasting Rock [the Rock of Ages].

ISAIAH 26:4

O my God, I trust, lean on, rely on, and am confident in You.

PSALM 25:2

DEVELOPING TRUST

How many times have you frustrated yourself and gotten all upset needlessly over trying situations that came your way? How many years of your life have you spent saying, "Oh, I'm believing God. I'm trusting God," when, in reality, all you were doing was worrying, talking negatively, and trying to figure out everything on your own? You may have thought you were trusting God because you were saying, "I trust God," but inside you were anxious and panicky. You were trying to learn to trust God, but you were not quite there yet.

Trust and confidence are built up over a period of time. It usually takes some time to overcome an ingrained habit of worry, anxiety, or fear. That is why it is so important to "hang in there" with God. Don't quit and give up, because you gain experience and spiritual strength every round you go through. Each time you become a little stronger than you were the last time. Sooner or later, if you don't give up, you will be more than the devil can handle.

*If you are in a time of trials, use that time
to build your trust in God. Trust Him to deliver you
or bring you through successfully.*

GOD'S WORD FOR YOU

Be well balanced. . . .

1 PETER 5:8

❧

You will guard him and keep him in perfect and constant peace whose mind [both its inclination and its character] is stayed on You, because he commits himself to You, leans on You, and hopes confidently in You.

ISAIAH 26:3

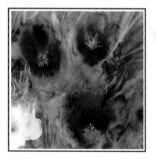

Be Well-Balanced

Sometimes in trying situations our anxiety gets in the way of our doing what we should. All we can do is our best, then trust God with the rest.

We function best when we have a calm, well-balanced mind. When our mind is calm, it is without fear, worry, or torment. When our mind is well-balanced, we are able to look the situation over and decide what to do or not to do about it.

Where most of us get in trouble is when we get out of balance. Either we move into a state of total passivity in which we do nothing, expecting God to do everything for us, or we become hyperactive, operating most of the time in the flesh. God wants us to be well-balanced so that we are able to face any situation of life and say, "Well, I believe I can do certain things about this situation, but no more."

Instead of getting distraught and full of fear and worry, we need to go before God and say, "Well, Lord, I'm believing You to help me in this situation, but is there something You want me to do?"

Whatever it is that God shows us to do about our problem, we need to be diligent enough to do it. Then we need to trust Him with the outcome.

Once we have done all we know to do,
we can trust God with the rest.
That is what I call faith and balance.

WHEN YOU FEEL INSECURE

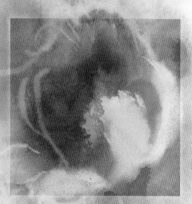

God is looking for people with
a right heart attitude toward Him,
not a perfect performance record.

GOD'S WORD FOR YOU

May you be rooted deep in love and founded securely on love,

That you may have the power and be strong to apprehend and grasp with all the saints [God's devoted people, the experience of that love] what is the breadth and length and height and depth [of it];

[That you may really come] to know [practically, through experience for yourselves] the love of Christ, which far surpasses mere knowledge [without experience]; that you may be filled [through all your being] unto all the fullness of God [may have the richest measure of the divine Presence, and become a body wholly filled and flooded with God Himself]!

EPHESIANS 3:17-19

four
WHEN YOU FEEL INSECURE

 any people have a deep feeling of insecurity about themselves because they can't accept themselves for who they are. Are you tired of playing games, wearing masks, trying to be someone other than who you are? Wouldn't you like the freedom just to be accepted as you are, without pressure to be someone you really don't know how to be?

God wants us to learn our value is not in what we do but in who we are in Him. He wants us to be willing to be who we are, weaknesses and all, because He accepts us unconditionally.

The devil's plan is to deceive us into basing our worth on our performance, then keep us focused on all our faults and shortcomings. Satan wants us to have a low opinion of ourselves so that we live ineffectively for God, being miserable and unreceptive to God's blessings because we don't think we deserve them.

It is so important to have a positive sense of self-esteem, self-value, and self-worth, to be secure in who we are in Christ, to truly like ourselves. We learn to like ourselves by learning how much God loves us. Once we become rooted and grounded in God's love, we can come to terms of peace with ourselves and stop feeling insecure.

Every one of us is imperfect,
and God loves us just the way we are.

GOD'S WORD FOR YOU

That the communication of thy faith may become effectual by the acknowledging of every good thing which is in you in Christ Jesus.

PHILEMON 1:6 KJV

❧

For by your words you will be justified and acquitted, and by your words you will be condemned and sentenced.

MATTHEW 12:37

ELIMINATE THE NEGATIVE

If we speak badly about ourselves, we will feel condemned. Let's apply what Jesus taught about our words as the first key to overcoming insecurity *and never speak negatively about ourselves*. We must speak words that empower us—not words that weaken us. If we want to increase our self-acceptance and our opinion of ourselves, we must decide that not one more negative comment about ourselves will ever come out of our mouth.

The devil wants us to acknowledge every bad trait we see in ourselves because he doesn't want the communication of our faith to be effectual. As the accuser of the brethren (Revelation 12:9-10), he continually tries to redirect our focus from who we are in Christ back on to our shortcomings.

We need to understand who we are in Christ and see how much He has done for us through shedding His blood to make us worthy. The communication of our faith is made effectual by acknowledging every *good thing* in us *in Christ Jesus*, not by acknowledging every *wrong thing* with *us*. Acts 10:15 says: "What God has cleansed and pronounced clean, do not you defile and profane by regarding and calling common and unhallowed or unclean."

Jesus was made perfect for us. Our acceptability to God is not based on our performance, but on our faith and trust in Jesus' performance.

GOD'S WORD FOR YOU

[Righteousness, standing acceptable to God] will be granted and credited to us also who believe in (trust in, adhere to, and rely on) God, Who raised Jesus our Lord from the dead.

ROMANS 4:24

∼✦∼

For our sake He made Christ [virtually] to be sin Who knew no sin, so that in and through Him we might become [endued with, viewed as being in, and examples of] the righteousness of God [what we ought to be, approved and acceptable and in right relationship with Him, by His goodness].

2 CORINTHIANS 5:21

Righteousness Is God's Gift

One of the first revelations God gave me out of the Word was on righteousness. By "revelation" I mean one day you suddenly understand something to the point that it becomes part of you. The knowledge isn't only in your mind—you no longer need to renew your mind to it because you don't wonder or hope it's true—you *know*.

Righteousness is God's gift to us. It is "imputed"— granted and credited—to us by virtue of our believing in what God did for us through His Son Jesus Christ. Jesus, Who knew no sin, became sin so that we might be made the righteousness of God in Jesus.

Above all else, the devil does not want us to walk in the reality that we are in right standing with God. He wants us to feel insecure, always vaguely contemplating what is wrong with us.

Jesus wants us to know that we are right with God because of what He has done for us. He wants us to live in His Kingdom and have peace and joy in the midst of every tribulation.

When we keep our eyes on the true Kingdom of God—on Him, His righteousness, His peace, and His joy—the rest will be added to us in abundance.

GOD'S WORD FOR YOU

For we all often stumble and fall and offend in many things. And if anyone does not offend in speech [never says the wrong things], he is a fully developed character and a perfect man, able to control his whole body and to curb his entire nature.

JAMES 3:2

Death and life are in the power of the tongue, and they who indulge in it shall eat the fruit of it [for death or life]. [Matt. 12:37.]

PROVERBS 18:21

CELEBRATE THE POSITIVE

A key to overcoming insecurity is this: *Meditate on and speak positive things about yourself.*

Our thoughts and words about ourselves are tremendously important. In order to overcome the negative thinking and speaking that have been such a natural part of our lifestyle for so long, we must make a conscious effort to think and speak good things about ourselves to ourselves by making positive confessions.

We need to get our mouth in line with what the Word of God says about us. Positive confession of the Word of God should be an ingrained habit of every believer. If you have not yet begun to develop this important habit, start today. Begin thinking and saying good things about yourself: "I am the righteousness of God in Jesus Christ. I prosper in everything I lay my hand to. I have gifts and talents, and God is using me. I operate in the fruit of the Spirit. I walk in love. Joy flows through me."

The Bible teaches we can appropriate the blessings of God in our lives by believing and confessing the positive things God has said about us in His Word.

If you will continually and purposefully speak about yourself what the Word of God says about you, you will receive positive results.

GOD'S WORD FOR YOU

He said this to indicate by what kind of death Peter would glorify God. And after this, He said to him, Follow Me!

But Peter turned and saw the disciple whom Jesus loved, following—the one who also had leaned back on His breast at the supper and had said, Lord, who is it that is going to betray You?

When Peter saw him, he said to Jesus, Lord, what about this man?

JOHN 21:19-21

VOID COMPARISONS

The next important key to overcoming insecurity is simple: *Never compare yourself with anyone else because it invites condemnation.*

I really want to encourage you to stop comparing yourself with other people about how you look, what position you occupy, or how long you pray. Comparison only thwarts God's working in your life.

We also must not compare our trials and tribulations to those of other people. Some situations may seem hard to you. But you cannot look at somebody else and say, "Why is all this happening to me and everything comes up roses for you?"

Jesus revealed to Peter ahead of time some of the suffering he would go through. Peter immediately wanted to compare his suffering and his lot in life with somebody else's by saying, "What about this man?"

"Jesus said to him, If I want him to stay (survive, live) till I come, what is that to you? [What concern is it of yours?] You follow Me!" (John 21:22).

That is His answer to us also. We are not called to compare, only to comply to His will for us.

God wants you to know that you are unique and that He has an individualized, specialized plan for your life.

GOD'S WORD FOR YOU

Having gifts (faculties, talents, qualities) that differ according to the grace given us, let us use them. . . .

ROMANS 12:6

✺

I have strength for all things in Christ Who empowers me [I am ready for anything and equal to anything through Him Who infuses inner strength into me; I am self-sufficient in Christ's sufficiency].

PHILIPPIANS 4:13

Focus on Potential, Not Limitations

In order to succeed at being yourself, build confidence, and overcome insecurity you must *focus on potential instead of limitations*. In other words, focus on your strengths instead of your weaknesses.

You and I really cannot do *anything* we want to do. We cannot do anything or everything that everyone else is doing. But we can do everything *God has called us to do*. And we can be anything *God says we can be*.

Each of us is full of gifts and talents and potentials and abilities. If we really begin to cooperate with God, we can go for the very best that God has for us. But if we get high-minded ideas and set goals that are beyond our abilities and the grace gifts on our life, we will become frustrated. We will not attain those goals, and we may even end up blaming God for our failure.

Gifts and talents are distributed by the Holy Spirit according to the grace that is on each person to handle them. If you are going to like yourself, if you are going to succeed at being yourself, you are going to have to focus on your potential—what God has created you to be—not on your limitations.

*If God has called you to do something,
you will find yourself loving it despite
any adversity that may beset you.*

GOD'S WORD FOR YOU

*Now am I trying to win the favor of men, or of God?
Do I seek to please men? If I were still seeking popularity
with men, I should not be a bond servant of Christ (the
Messiah).*

GALATIANS 1:10

∽

*Not with eyeservice, as menpleasers; but as the
servants of Christ, doing the will of God from the heart.*

EPHESIANS 6:6 KJV

Have the Courage to Be Different

If you are going to overcome insecurity and be the person you are called to be in Christ, *you must have the courage to be different*. To be a success at being completely and fully you, you are going to have to take a chance on not being like everyone else.

Becoming menpleasers is one of the easiest things we can do but one that can ultimately make us very unhappy. When we begin pleasing other people, we begin to hear comments that make us feel good about ourselves. That is okay as long as we do not derive our sense of worth from it. As believers, our sense of worth has to be rooted and grounded in the love of God.

We are worth something because God sent His only Son to die for us. We are worth something because God loves us, not because of what everybody else thinks about us or says about us.

As followers of Christ, we are to be led by the Spirit, not controlled by people, doing what everybody else wants us to do because we think that will gain us acceptance and approval. In the same manner, we should not try to control others, but allow them to be led by the Spirit just as we are.

Don't put God in a box. He has many ways of leading you if you will permit Him to be the Leader while you become the follower.

GOD'S WORD FOR YOU

But as for you, the anointing (the sacred appointment, the unction) which you received from Him abides [permanently] in you; [so] then you have no need that anyone should instruct you. But just as His anointing teaches you concerning everything and is true and is no falsehood, so you must abide in (live in, never depart from) Him [being rooted in Him, knit to Him], just as [His anointing] has taught you [to do].

1 JOHN 2:27 TLB

ℒEARN TO COPE WITH CRITICISM

If you are going to overcome insecurity, you have *to learn to cope with criticism.*

Are you a self-validating person, or do you need outside validation? Outside validation is needing somebody to tell you that you are okay. Self-validation is taking action as you are led by the Holy Ghost.

When we hear from God, we often confer too much with people. With the Holy Spirit in us, we do not need to consult with others. The writer of Proverbs says, "In the multitude of counselors there is safety" (Proverbs 11:14). The answer is to be obedient to the Spirit without refusing counsel from others who are wiser than we are.

We must learn to be secure enough to know how to cope with criticism without feeling there is something wrong with us. We must not come under bondage thinking we have to conform to other people's opinions.

Have enough confidence in who you are in Christ that you can listen to others and be open to change without feeling you have to agree with their viewpoint or meet with their approval if you don't feel their suggestion is right for you.

❧

You may have faults, there may be things about you that need to be changed, but God is working on you the same as He is on everybody else.

GOD'S WORD FOR YOU

For we [Christians] are the true circumcision, who worship God in spirit and by the Spirit of God and exult and glory and pride ourselves in Jesus Christ, and put no confidence or dependence [on what we are] in the flesh and on outward privileges and physical advantages and external appearances.

PHILIPPIANS 3:3

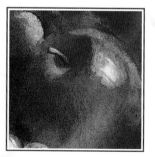

DISCOVER THE TRUE SOURCE OF CONFIDENCE

The most important key to becoming more secure is *to discover the true source of confidence.* In what do you place your confidence? That question must be settled before you can ever have God's confidence. Before your confidence can be in Him, you must remove your confidence from other things.

Is God dealing with you about where you have placed your confidence? Is it in marriage? A college degree? Your job? Your spouse? Your children?

We should not place our confidence in our education, our looks, our position, our gifts, our talents, or in other people's opinions. Our heavenly Father is saying to us, "No more; it is time to let go of all those fleshly things you have been holding so firmly for so long. It is time to put your trust and confidence in Me, and Me alone!"

You must come to the place where your confidence is not in the flesh but in Christ Jesus. Learn to trust Him: "Commit your way to the Lord [roll and repose each care of your load on Him]; trust (lean on, rely on, and be confident) also in Him and He will bring it to pass" (Psalm 37:5).

Allow the Lord to shake loose from you the false sense of confidence, worth, security, and well-being you are trying so hard to derive from earthly things.

WHEN
YOU FEEL
DEPRESSED

To live as God intends for us to live,
the first thing we must do
is truly believe that it is God's will
for us to experience continual joy.

God's Word for You

I waited patiently and expectantly for the Lord; and He inclined to me and heard my cry.

He drew me up out of a horrible pit [a pit of tumult and of destruction], out of the miry clay (froth and slime), and set my feet upon a rock, steadying my steps and establishing my goings.

And He has put a new song in my mouth, a song of praise to our God. Many shall see and fear (revere and worship) and put their trust and confident reliance in the Lord. [Ps. 5:11].

PSALM 40:1-3

❧

Be glad in the Lord and rejoice, you [uncompromisingly] righteous [you who are upright and in right standing with Him]; shout for joy, all you upright in heart!

PSALM 32:11

❧

five
WHEN YOU FEEL DEPRESSED

People from all walks of life have bouts with depression. There are many underlying causes for depression and a variety of treatments offered to deal with it. Some are effective, but many are not. Some help temporarily but can never permanently remove the torment of depression. The good news is that Jesus can heal depression and deliver us from it.

God has given us His joy to fight depression. If you are a believer in Jesus Christ, the joy of the Lord is inside you. Many believers know this but don't have the slightest idea how to tap into that joy or release it. We need to experience what is ours as a result of our faith in Jesus Christ. *It is God's will for us to experience joy!*

I had problems with depression myself a long time ago. But, thank God, I learned I didn't have to allow the negative feeling of depression to rule me. I learned how to release the joy of the Lord in my life!

No matter what you have gone through in life or are going through now, if you are a believer in Jesus Christ, you have His joy inside you, and you can learn how to release it to win over depression.

The reason we can laugh and enjoy life in spite of our current situation or circumstances is because Jesus is our joy.

GOD'S WORD FOR YOU

. . . but one thing I do [it is my one aspiration]; forgetting what lies behind and straining forward to what lies ahead.

PHILIPPIANS 3:13

DEAL WITH DISAPPOINTMENT

All of us must face and deal with disappointment at different times. No person alive has everything happen in life the way they want in the way they expect.

When things don't prosper or succeed according to our plan, the first emotion we feel is disappointment. This is normal. There is nothing wrong with feeling disappointed. But we must know what to do with that feeling, or it will move into something more serious.

In the world we cannot live without experiencing disappointment, but in Jesus we can always be given re-appointment!

The apostle Paul stated that one important lesson he had learned in life was to let go of what lay behind and press toward all that lay ahead!

When we get disappointed, then immediately get re-appointed, that's exactly what we're doing. We're letting go of the causes for the disappointment and pressing toward what God has for us. We get a new vision, plan, idea, a fresh outlook, a new mind-set, and we change our focus to that. *We decide to go on!*

Every day is a brand-new start! We can let go of yesterday's disappointments and give God a chance to do something wonderful for us today.

GOD'S WORD FOR YOU

*But about midnight, as Paul and Silas were praying
and singing hymns of praise to God. . . . Suddenly there
was a great earthquake, so that the very foundations of the
prison were shaken; and at once all the doors were opened
and everyone's shackles were unfastened.*

ACTS 16:25-26

❧

*Rejoice in the Lord always [delight, gladden yourselves
in Him]; again I say, Rejoice!*

PHILIPPIANS 4:4

THE POWER OF REJOICING

Throughout the Bible, God instructs His people to be filled with joy and rejoice. The apostle Paul, inspired by the Holy Spirit, instructed the Philippians twice to rejoice. Any time the Lord tells us twice to do something, we need to pay careful attention to what He is saying.

Many times people see or hear the word "rejoice" and say, "That sounds nice, but how do I do that?" They would like to rejoice but don't know how!

Paul and Silas, who had been beaten, thrown into prison, and their feet put in stocks, rejoiced by simply singing praises to God. They chose to rejoice, despite their circumstances.

The same power that opened the doors and broke the shackles off Paul and Silas and those imprisoned with them is available to people today who are imprisoned and shackled with depression.

Joy can be anything from calm delight to extreme hilarity. Joy improves our countenance, our health, and the quality of our lives. It strengthens our witness to others and makes some of the less desirable circumstances in life more bearable.

GOD'S WORD FOR YOU

. . . for the joy of the Lord is your strength and stronghold.

NEHEMIAH 8:10

❦

But none of these things move me; neither do I esteem my life dear to myself, if only I may finish my course with joy and the ministry which I have obtained from [which was entrusted to me by] the Lord Jesus, faithfully to attest to the good news (Gospel) of God's grace (His unmerited favor, spiritual blessing, and mercy).

ACTS 20:24

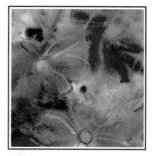

Prime the Pump

When we don't feel joyful, we need to take some action to release joy before we start slipping into depression. Sometimes we must start to rejoice whether we feel like it or not. It is like priming a pump by repeatedly moving the handle up and down until the pump kicks in and the water begins to flow.

I remember my grandparents had an old-time pump. I can recall standing at the sink as a small child moving the pump handle up and down and sometimes feeling as though it would never take hold and start to supply water. It actually felt as if it was connected to nothing, and I was just pumping air.

But if I didn't give up, moving the handle up and down would soon become more difficult. That was a sign that water would start flowing shortly.

This is the way it is with joy. We have a well of water on the inside of our spirit. The pump handle to bring it up is physical exuberance—smiling, singing, laughing, and so forth. At first the physical expressions may not seem to be doing any good. And after a while it even gets harder, but if we keep it up, soon we will get a "gusher" of joy.

If joy is a fruit of the Spirit,
and the Spirit is in you, joy is in you.
What we need to do is learn how to release it.

GOD'S WORD FOR YOU

Why are you cast down, O my inner self? And why should you moan over me and be disquieted within me? Hope in God and wait expectantly for Him, for I shall yet praise Him, my Help and my God.

PSALM 42:5

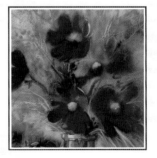

WAIT EXPECTANTLY FOR GOD

Does your inner man ever feel cast down? Sometimes mine does. So did David's. When he felt that way, David put his hope in God and waited for Him, praising Him as his Help and his God.

To overcome his downcast feelings and emotions, he used songs and shouts of deliverance. That's why so many of his psalms are songs of praise to God to be sung in the midst of unsettling situations.

David knew that when he got down, his countenance went down with him. That is why he talked to himself, his soul (mind, will, and emotions), and encouraged and strengthened himself in the Lord (1 Samuel 30:6).

When we find ourselves in that same depressed state—we should wait expectantly for the Lord, praise Him Who is our Help and our God, and encourage and strengthen ourselves in Him.

We who are righteous—in right standing with God—by believing in Jesus Christ, we who take refuge and put our trust in the Lord can sing and shout for joy! The Lord makes a covering over us and defends us. He fights our battles for us when we praise Him (2 Chronicles 20:17, 20-21)!

You and I must realize and remember that depression is not part of our inheritance in Jesus Christ. It is not part of God's will for His children.

GOD'S WORD FOR YOU

Be well balanced (temperate, sober of mind), be vigilant and cautious at all times; for that enemy of yours, the devil, roams around like a lion roaring [in fierce hunger], seeking someone to seize upon and devour.

Withstand him; be firm in faith [against his onset— rooted, established, strong, immovable, and determined], knowing that the same (identical) sufferings are appointed to your brotherhood (the whole body of Christians) throughout the world.

1 PETER 5:8-9

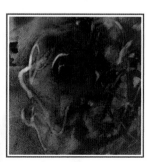

RESIST DEPRESSION IMMEDIATELY

There are many causes of depression—but only one source: Satan. He wants to keep us pressed down and feeling badly about ourselves so that we won't receive all that Jesus died to give us.

No matter what the causes of depression—physical, mental, emotional, or spiritual—as soon as we feel depression coming on, we need to resist it immediately and take whatever action the Lord leads us to take.

Don't play around with depression. As soon as we start feeling disappointed, we must say to ourselves, "I had better do something about this before it gets worse." If we don't, we will ultimately get discouraged, then depressed. Jesus gave us "the garment of praise for the spirit of heaviness" to put on (Isaiah 61:3 KJV). If we don't use what He has given us, we will sink lower and lower into the pit of depression and could end up in real trouble.

Resisting Satan at his onset will stop extended bouts of depression. We resist the devil by submitting ourselves to God and by wielding the sword of the Spirit, which is His Word (Ephesians 6:17).

Anytime we feel anything that is not part of the will of God for us, that is when we need to begin to wield the sharp, two-edged sword of the Word.

GOD'S WORD FOR YOU

Therefore, [there is] now no condemnation (no adjudging guilty of wrong) for those who are in Christ Jesus, who live [and] walk not after the dictates of the flesh, but after the dictates of the Spirit. [John 3:18.]

ROMANS 8:1

No Condemnation

One of the biggest tools Satan uses to try to make us feel bad is condemnation, which certainly can be a cause of depression. According to this scripture, we who are in Christ Jesus are no longer condemned, no longer judged guilty or wrong. Yet so often we judge and condemn ourselves.

Until I learned and understood the Word of God, I lived a large part of my life feeling guilty. If someone had asked me what I felt guilty about, I could not have answered. All I knew was that there was a vague feeling of guilt that followed me around all the time.

From that experience, God gave me a real revelation about walking free from guilt and condemnation. He showed me that you and I must not only receive forgiveness from Him, we must also forgive ourselves. We must stop beating ourselves over the head for something that He has forgiven and forgotten (Jeremiah 31:34; Acts 10:15).

I believe it is nearly impossible to get depressed if the mind is kept under strict control. That is why we are told in Isaiah 26:3 that God will guard and keep us in perfect and constant peace—if we will keep our mind stayed on Him.

God has new things on the horizon
of your life, but you will never see them
if you live in and relive the past.

GOD'S WORD FOR YOU

*Although my father and my mother have forsaken me,
yet the Lord will take me up [adopt me as His child].*

PSALM 27:10

❧

*See what [an incredible] quality of love the Father has
given (shown, bestowed on) us, that we should [be
permitted to] be named and called and counted the
children of God! And so we are!*

1 JOHN 3:1

GOD DOES NOT REJECT US

Rejection causes depression. To be rejected means to be thrown away as having no value or as being unwanted. We were created for acceptance, not rejection. The emotional pain of rejection is one of the deepest kinds known. Especially if the rejection comes from someone we love or expect to love us, like parents or a spouse.

If you have been depressed, it might be due to a root of rejection in your life. Overcoming rejection is certainly not easy, but we can overcome it through the love of Jesus Christ.

In Ephesians 3:18, Paul prayed for the church that they would know "the breadth and length and height and depth" of the love that God had for them and that they would experience it for themselves. He said this experience far surpasses mere knowledge.

Watch for all the ways that God shows His love for you, and it will overcome the rejection you may have experienced from other people. Every time God gives us favor, He is showing us that He loves us. There are many ways He shows His love for us all the time; we simply need to begin watching for it.

Having a deep revelation concerning God's love for us will keep us from depression.

GOD'S WORD FOR YOU

To the praise of the glory of his grace, wherein he hath made us accepted in the beloved.

EPHESIANS 1:6 KJV

LISTEN TO WHAT GOD SAYS ABOUT YOU

God does not want us to feel frustrated and condemned. He wants us to realize that we are pleasing to Him just as we are.

The devil keeps trying to tell us what we are not, but God keeps trying to tell us what we are—His beloved children who are well-pleasing to Him.

God never reminds us of how far we have fallen. He always reminds us of how far we have risen. He reminds us of how much we have overcome, how precious we are in His sight, how much He loves us.

The devil tells us we cannot possibly be acceptable to God because we are not perfect, but God tells us that we are accepted in the Beloved because of what He has already done for us.

God wants us to know that His hand is upon us, that His angels are watching over us, that His Holy Spirit is right there in us and with us to help us in everything we do.

He wants us to know that Jesus is our Friend, and that as we walk with Him day by day, good things are going to take place in our lives.

If we listen to God rather than the devil,
He will give us peace about the past,
joy for the present, and hope for the future.

WHEN
YOU FEEL
AFRAID

We can live without fear
by building our faith on what
God has said in His Word.

GOD'S WORD FOR YOU

*Fear not [there is nothing to fear], for I am with you;
do not look around you in terror and be dismayed, for I
am your God. I will strengthen and harden you to
difficulties, yes, I will help you; yes, I will hold you up
and retain you with My [victorious] right hand of rightness
and justice.*

ISAIAH 41:10

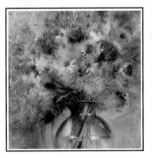

six

WHEN YOU FEEL AFRAID

 ne of the benefits available to us in our spiritual inheritance as a believer in Jesus Christ is freedom from fear. But even if we are afraid, we know that we can go ahead and act on what God says, because God will be with us to protect us. He will help us, go before to fight the battle for us or deliver us, bringing us through victoriously as we obey Him.

If you feel you have missed out on some blessings in your life because of fear, you can learn how to handle or overcome fear and begin to experience the abundant life God has planned for you.

The message of "fear not, for I, the Lord, am with you" is expressed in many different ways throughout the Bible. God does not want us to fear because fear prevents us from receiving and doing all He has planned for us. He loves us and wants to bless us, and He has provided ways for us not to fear.

The only acceptable attitude (and confession) that a Christian can have toward fear is this: "It is not from God, and I will not let it control my life! I will confront fear, for it is a spirit sent out from hell to torment me."

God has a plan for your life. Receive His plan by putting your faith in Him. Make a decision today that you will no longer let a spirit of fear intimidate you and dominate your life.

Jesus is your Deliverer. As you diligently seek Him, He will deliver you from all fear.

GOD'S WORD FOR YOU

*Fear not; stand still (firm, confident, undismayed)
and see the salvation of the Lord which He will work for
you today.*

EXODUS 14:13

❧

*. . . the devil . . . was a murderer from the beginning
and does not stand in the truth, because there is no truth
in him. When he speaks a falsehood, he speaks what is
natural to him, for he is a liar [himself] and the father of
lies and of all that is false.*

JOHN 8:44

FEAR IS FALSEHOOD

Jesus said that the devil is a liar and the father of all lies. The truth is not in him. He tries to use falsehood to deceive God's people into fear so they will not be bold enough to be obedient to the Lord and reap the blessings He has in store for them.

Often the fear of something is worse than the thing itself. If we will be courageous and determined to do whatever it is we fear, we will discover it is not nearly as bad as we thought it would be.

Throughout the Word of God we find the Lord saying to His people, "Fear not." I believe the reason He did that was to encourage them so they would not allow Satan to rob them of their blessing.

In the same way, because He knows we are fearful, the Lord continues to exhort and encourage us to press through what lies before us to do His will. Why? Because He knows that great blessings await us.

Fear, which is spelled f-e-a-r, stands for *false evidence appearing real*. The enemy wants to tell you that your current situation is evidence that your future will be a failure, but the Bible teaches us that no matter what our present circumstances, nothing is impossible with God (Mark 9:17-23).

Only when you know God's Word will you recognize the lies of Satan. Confess the Word of God, and it will bring you into a place of victory.

GOD'S WORD FOR YOU

For God did not give us a spirit of timidity (of cowardice, of craven and cringing and fawning fear), but [He has given us a spirit] of power and of love and of calm and well-balanced mind and discipline and self-control.

2 TIMOTHY 1:7

No Fear!

Every one of us has experienced starting to step out in faith, and even at the thought of it, fear begins to rise up in us. We need to realize that the source of fear is Satan. First John 4:18 KJV says: "There is no fear in love; but perfect love casteth out fear: because fear hath torment. He that feareth is not made perfect in love."

Satan sends fear to try to torment us into being so doubtful and miserable so that we will be prevented from doing what God wants us to do and receiving all that God has for us.

We can live without fear by building our faith on what God has said in His Word. When we open our mouth and confess what the Lord says to us and about us, God's Word will give us the power to overcome the fears that torment and prevent.

When we find ourselves trying to avoid confronting some issue in our life because of fear or dread or wondering or reasoning, we should pray and ask God to do for us what He has promised in His Word—to go before us and pave the way for us.

Ask God to strengthen you in the inner man, that His might and power may fill you, and that you may not be overcome with the temptation to give in to fear.

GOD'S WORD FOR YOU

For [the Spirit which] you have now received [is] not a spirit of slavery to put you once more in bondage to fear, but you have received the Spirit of adoption [the Spirit producing sonship] in [the bliss of] which we cry, Abba (Father)! Father!

ROMANS 8:15

I WILL NOT FEAR!

Fear robs many people of their faith.

Fear of failure, fear of man, and fear of rejection are some of the strongest fears employed by Satan to hinder us from making progress. But no matter what kind of fear the enemy sends against us, the important thing is to overcome it. When we are faced with fear, we must not give in to it. It is imperative to our victory that we determine, "I will not fear!"

The normal reaction to fear is flight. Satan wants us to run; God wants us to stand still and see His deliverance.

Because of fear, many people do not confront issues; they spend their lives running. We must learn to stand our ground and face fear, secure in the knowledge that we are more than conquerors (Romans 8:37).

Fear of failure torments multitudes. We fear what people will think of us if we fail. If we step out and fail, some people may hear about it; but they quickly forget if we forget it and go on. It is better to try something and fail than to try nothing and succeed.

Approach life with boldness. The Spirit of the Lord is in you — so make up your mind not to fear.

GOD'S WORD FOR YOU

The earnest (heartfelt, continued) prayer of a righteous man makes tremendous power available [dynamic in its working].

JAMES 5:16

PRAY ABOUT EVERYTHING AND FEAR NOTHING

Some time ago the Lord spoke these words to me: "Pray about everything and fear nothing." Over the next couple of weeks, He showed me different things about prayer versus fear. Many of them dealt with little areas in which fear would try to creep into my life and cause me problems. He showed me that in every case, no matter how great or important or how small or insignificant, the solution was to pray.

Sometimes we become afraid by staring at our circumstances. The more we focus on the problem, the more fearful we become. Instead, we are to keep our focus on God. He is able to handle anything that we may ever have to face in this life.

God has promised to strengthen us, to harden us to difficulties, to hold us up and retain us with His victorious right hand. He also commands us not to be afraid. But remember, He is not commanding us never to feel fear, but rather not to let it control us.

The Lord is saying to you and me personally, "Fear not, I will help you." But we never experience the help of God until we place everything on the line, until we are obedient enough to step out in faith.

When you feel fear, don't back down or run away. Instead, pray and go forward even though you are afraid.

GOD'S WORD FOR YOU

If any of you is deficient in wisdom, let him ask of the giving God [Who gives] to everyone liberally and ungrudgingly, without reproaching or faultfinding, and it will be given him.

Only it must be in faith that he asks with no wavering (no hesitating, no doubting). For the one who wavers (hesitates, doubts) is like the billowing surge out at sea that is blown hither and thither and tossed by the wind.

For truly, let not such a person imagine that he will receive anything [he asks for] from the Lord.

JAMES 1:5-7

FAITH: THE ANTIDOTE FOR FEAR

Faith is the only antidote for fear.

If you or I drank some kind of poison, we would have to swallow an antidote, or the poison would cause serious damage or even death. The same is true of the deadly toxin of fear. There must be an antidote for it, and the only antidote for fear is faith.

When fear comes knocking at our door, we must answer it with faith, because nothing else is effective against it. And prayer is the major vehicle that carries faith.

Faith must be carried to the problem and released in some way. It is possible to pray without faith (we do it all the time), but it is impossible to have real faith and *not* pray.

James tells us that when we find ourselves in need of something, we should pray and ask God for it in *simple, believing* prayer. Those two words are very important. The way we do that is by simply praying and having faith, believing that what we ask for from God we will receive in accordance with His divine will and plan.

Put your faith in the Lord.
He has the power to deliver you from all fear.

GOD'S WORD FOR YOU

Now [in Haran] the Lord said to Abram, Go for yourself [for your own advantage] away from your country, from your relatives and your father's house, to the land that I will show you.

GENESIS 12:1

DO IT AFRAID!

How would you feel if God told you to leave your home, your family, and everything familiar and comfortable to you and head out to who knows where? Full of fear? That is precisely the challenge Abram faced, and it frightened him. That's why God kept saying to him again and again, "Fear not."

Elisabeth Elliot, whose husband was killed along with four other missionaries in Ecuador, tells that her life was controlled completely by fear. Every time she started to step out, fear stopped her. A friend told her something that set her free. She said, "Why don't you do it afraid?" Elisabeth Elliot and Rachel Saint, sister of one of the murdered missionaries, went on to evangelize the Indian tribes, including the people who had killed their husband and brother.

If we wait to do something until we are not afraid, we will probably accomplish very little for God, others, or even for ourselves. Both Abram and Joshua had to step out in faith and obedience to God and do what He had commanded them to do—afraid. We must do the same!

Be determined that your life is not going to be ruled by fear but by God's Word.

GOD'S WORD FOR YOU

After these things, the word of the Lord came to Abram in a vision, saying, Fear not, Abram, I am your Shield, your abundant compensation, and your reward shall be exceedingly great.

GENESIS 15:1

Courage and Obedience Produce Great Rewards

In Genesis 12:1, God gave Abram a tall order. In so many words He said, "Pack up and leave everyone you know and everything you are comfortable with and go to a place I will show you."

If Abram had bowed his knee to fear, the rest of the story would never have come to pass. He would never have experienced God as his Shield, his great compensation, and he would never have received his exceedingly great reward.

In the same way, if Joshua had not overcome his fear and been obedient to God's command to lead His people into the Promised Land, neither he nor they would ever have enjoyed all that God had planned and prepared for them.

There is power in God's Word to equip us to stop bowing our knee in fear to the devil's desires. We can do what God wants us to do, even if we have to do it afraid. We need to keep saying: "Lord, strengthen me. This is what You have told me to do, and with Your help I am going to do it, because it is Your revealed will for me. I am determined that my life is not going to be ruled by fear but by Your Word."

✻

God doesn't always deliver us "from" things;
often He walks us "through" them.

GOD'S WORD FOR YOU

So we take comfort and are encouraged and confidently and boldly say, The Lord is my Helper; I will not be seized with alarm [I will not fear or dread or be terrified]. What can man do to me?

HEBREWS 13:6

Combat Fear With Prayer

Fear attacks everyone. It is Satan's way of tormenting us and preventing us from enjoying the life Jesus died to give us. If we accept the fears that Satan offers and give voice to them, we open the door for the enemy and close the door to God.

We must learn as David and the writer of Hebrews to boldly confess that God is our Helper, our Refuge, and our Stronghold.

Satan seeks to weaken us through fear, but God strengthens us as we fellowship with Him in prayer. The Bible teaches us to watch and pray: "All of you must keep awake (give strict attention, be cautious and active) and watch and pray, that you may not come into temptation. The spirit indeed is willing, but the flesh is weak" (Matthew 26:41). The major reference in this passage is to watching ourselves and the attacks that the enemy launches against our minds and our emotions. When these attacks are detected, we should pray immediately. We must remember that it is when we pray that power is released against the enemy—not when we think about praying later.

Watch and pray about everything. I believe you will find this decision to be one that will produce more joy and peace for your everyday living.

If we are ever to have real victory over the enemy, we must resist him in prayer with faith.

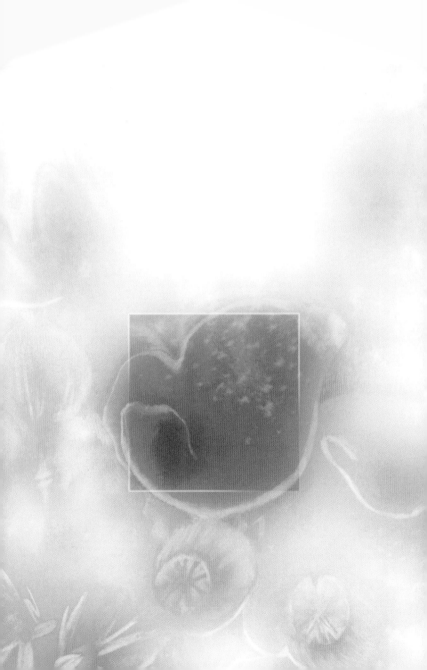

JOYCE MEYER is one of the world's leading practical Bible teachers. A #1 *New York Times* bestselling author, she has written more than seventy inspirational books, including *The Confident Woman*, *I Dare You*, the entire Battlefield of the Mind family of books, her first venture into fiction with *The Penny*, and many others. She has also released thousands of audio teachings as well as a complete video library. Joyce's *Enjoying Everyday Life*® radio and television programs are broadcast around the world, and she travels extensively conducting conferences. Joyce and her husband, Dave, are the parents of four grown children and make their home in St. Louis, Missouri.

TO CONTACT THE AUTHOR,
PLEASE WRITE:

Joyce Meyer Ministries
P.O. Box 655
Fenton, MO 63026
USA
(636) 349-0303
www.joycemeyer.org

Joyce Meyer Ministries—Canada
Lambeth Box 1300
London, ON N6P 1T5
Canada
1-800-727-9673

Joyce Meyer Ministries—Australia
Locked Bag 77
Mansfield Delivery Centre
Queensland 4122
Australia
(07) 3349 1200

Joyce Meyer Ministries—England
P.O. Box 1549
Windsor SL4 1GT
United Kingdom
01753 831102

Joyce Meyer Ministries—South Africa
P.O. Box 5
Cape Town 8000
South Africa
(27) 21-701-1056